Henschel Hs 129
Krzysztof Wołowski

In memory of the late Krzysztof Wołowski.

I0894120

Introduction

In 1937, the *Technische Amt* issued a specification for a cannon-armed close-support aircraft, small in size but heavily armoured. The final competing aircraft were the Focke-Wulf and the Henschel designs.

In September 1938, both companies received development contracts for three prototypes of each model. Focke-Wulf's project did not receive a separate designation, being based on an already approved model, the 8-189 ('8' was the RLM code for engine-powered aircraft), therefore the assault version was officially called Fw 189 S (S for *Schlacht*, or battle). Henschel secured for their original design a new RLM List Number, 8-129, thus its ground attack aircraft project became the Hs 129.

As soon as the RLM orders had been issued, preparation for production started at both Focke-Wulf's Bremen and Henschel's Schönefeld plants. Metal was cut in early October 1938, the initial prototypes (V1b for the Fw 189 and V1 for the Hs 129) taking shape by the end of the year. The overall light grey painted Hs 129 V1, carrying civilian markings D-ONUD, first took off on 26 May 1939, on the company's Schönefeld grounds. This was a few weeks after the Focke-Wulf 189 V1b's initial flight. The two competing prototypes had further different drawbacks, too. While the Henschel 129's particularity was the cramped cockpit, Focke-Wulf's design suffered from a higher overall weight, which further diminished the already inadequate manoeuvrability. With the extensive flight trials in progress, the balance started to tip slightly in favour of the Henschel design. The Hs 129 V2 (W.Nr. 129 3002) had been completed at Schönefeld, and had taken to the air on 30 November 1939. This second prototype did not last long, as it was destroyed during a test flight on 5 January 1940. The Hs 129 V2 was followed by the V3 (W.Nr. 129 3003). The maiden flight was again delayed due to the unavailability of the engines and propellers. Therefore the V3 was first flown only on 2 April 1940. The V3 then joined the V1 at E-Stelle Rechlin. In the meantime, V1 had received TF+AM Stammkennzeichen (Radio Code), a system introduced in the Luftwaffe from 18 October 1939 on. V3 became TF+AO.

Parallel to the ongoing evaluation and operational tests in July 1940, Henschel started the production of twenty-three A-0 pre-series aircraft, ordered by the RLM. Production was to be completed by November 1940. These airframes were tentatively assigned the W.Nr. 129 3004 to 129 3026 batch. The first A-0 received the Luftwaffe radio code GM+OA, the remaining A-0s being assigned with the rest of the series. Maiden flight of the first A-0 was on 1 August 1940. In September 1940, the RLM reduced the number of A-0s to twelve (W.Nr. 129 3004–129 3015, GM+OA to GM+OL), while the additionally ordered 16 A-1s were to be refitted with more powerful engines and subsequently assigned with a new pre-series sub-type, the B-0. This latter batch received a new Werknummer block as well, 0016 to 0031 instead of 129 3016 to 129 3031, and was planned to be delivered between February to May 1941. This deadline could not be kept, however, as the last A-0 rolled off the production line only in May 1941. Eventually, the B-0 pre-series was completed only in the first month of 1942, an eight-month delay.

In the autumn of 1940, the first completed A-0s were delivered to a specialised unit, namely 5. (*Schlacht*) *Staffel* (5th Ground Attack Squadron) of *Lehrgeschwader* 2 (LG 2, or the 2nd Operational Development Wing), based at Tutow, for trials under service conditions. Seven Hs 129A-0s were taken on charge by the end of the year. Seasoned test pilots were far from being satisfied with the Hs 129A. Despite the improvements already implemented by Henschel, the main complaints remained the same as previously mentioned by the E-Stelle test pilots: poor visibility, low engine power and average handling characteristics.

In early 1941, the ongoing order had been changed, yet again, by the RLM. The new request called for 60 Hs 129A-1/14M. The suffix after the Hs 129's sub-type designation represented the type of replacement powerplant finally settled upon by the RLM, namely the Gnome-Rhône 14M 04/05 radial. The French engine was rated at 700 hp (522 kW), the maximum take off power at 3030 rpm, which represented a 50% increase compared to the earlier Argus in-line engine.

As a consequence, Henschel Flugzeug-Werke A. G. was ordered to adapt the existing Hs 129A-1 airframes to accommodate the selected new French engine type. The upgraded cockpit design had to be included in the new design as well, as it significantly increased the pilot's all-around visibility, clearing one of the main complaints of the test pilots. Except for the ten A-1s already in manufacture, the rest of the initial order calling for 60 airframes was, temporarily, suspended.he previous order calling for the 16 original Argus-powered A-1s was maintained; however, the airframes were to be re-engined with the Gnome-Rhône 14M radials. The new batch, now renamed B-0s, was assigned with Stammkennzeichen KK+VI to KK+VX (W. Nr. 0016 to 0031). The B-0 series was later on expanded to 27 aircraft (W. Nr. 0016 to 0042).As a step to optimising manufacture, the wing leading edge was straightened and the trailing edge also followed a straight, tapering line. As a consequence, wing surface area increased slightly, from 28.40 m2 to 29.00 m2. The fuselage nose was enlarged and slightly rounded, offering an aerodynamically cleaner profile. The cockpit enclosure was completely redesigned. To significantly improve the pilot's view, the earlier, V-shaped, two-piece windshield was changed to an enlarged, slightly curved, single piece unit. According to an RAF crash report of a B-2 sub-type found in Africa, the windshield was made up by four layers of curved laminated glass, of the following thicknesses: 4½ mm, 5½ mm, 17 mm and 4½ mm. This gives a total thickness, including the cementing layers, of 55½ mm. A sheet of 6 mm Triplex glass was mounted behind the bulletproof screen, with an air space of 10 mm between the two screens. Hot air could be passed between the screens for de-misting purposes. The area of the side glass panels was doubled and they were modified to allow them to be opened and slid rearwards, allowing the pilot to reach out, if needed.

With all modifications completed, it can be stated that the end result, the 'Berta', was a significantly better machine than its predecessor, the 'Anton'. The first complete aircraft to be modified to test the improvements incorporated into the B-0 series was Hs 129A-0, W. Nr. 129 3007, GM+OD. Production of

Continued at the last page.

1

Hs 129 V3/U1, W.Nr. 3003, SKZ FT+AO.

Standard camouflage RLM 70/71/65 with distinctive red & white sharkmouth typical for A-0 series.

2

Hs 129A-0 W.Nr. 3016, SKZ GM+OM, possibly 5./SG 101.

Standard camouflage 70/71/65. Spinner tips red with white band.

3

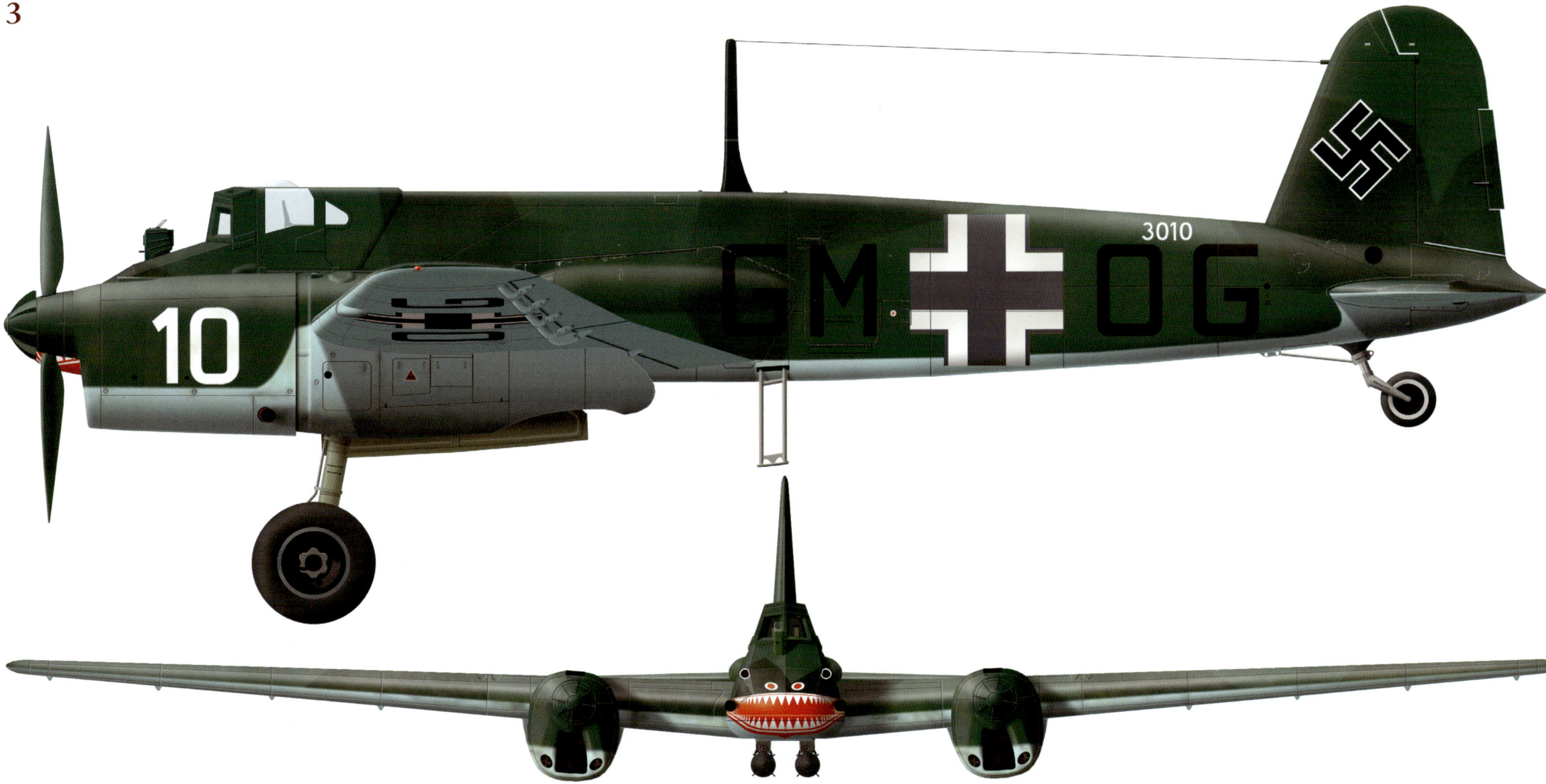

Hs 129A-0 W.Nr. 3010, SKZ GM+OG, possibly 4./SG 101.

Standard camouflage 70/71/65. The a/c was heavily damaged (65%) at Clermont-Ferrand airfield on 30th April, 1944.

4

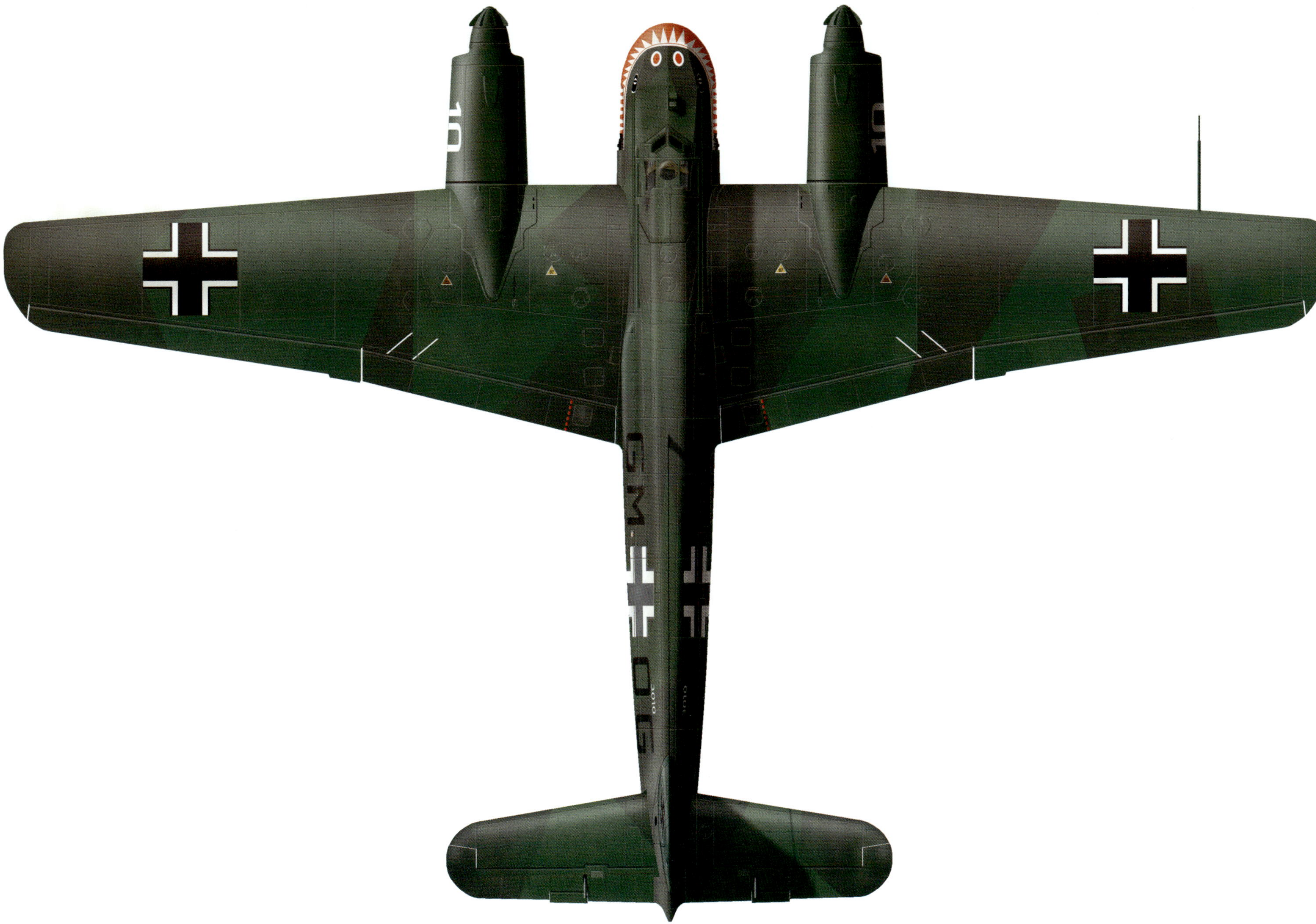

5

Hs 129A-0 W.Nr. 3010, SKZ GM+OG, possibly 4./SG 101.

6

7

Hs 129B-0 W.Nr. 0021, SKZ KK+VN.

Standard camouflage 70/71/65, upper surfaces of wings and horizontal tailplane painted RLM 02 and partially worn.

Note the absence of cooling vents on upper engine cowling.

On 29th September, 1942 the a/c crashed near Dęblin-Irena due to engine damage with Fw. Hans Hauer KIA.

8

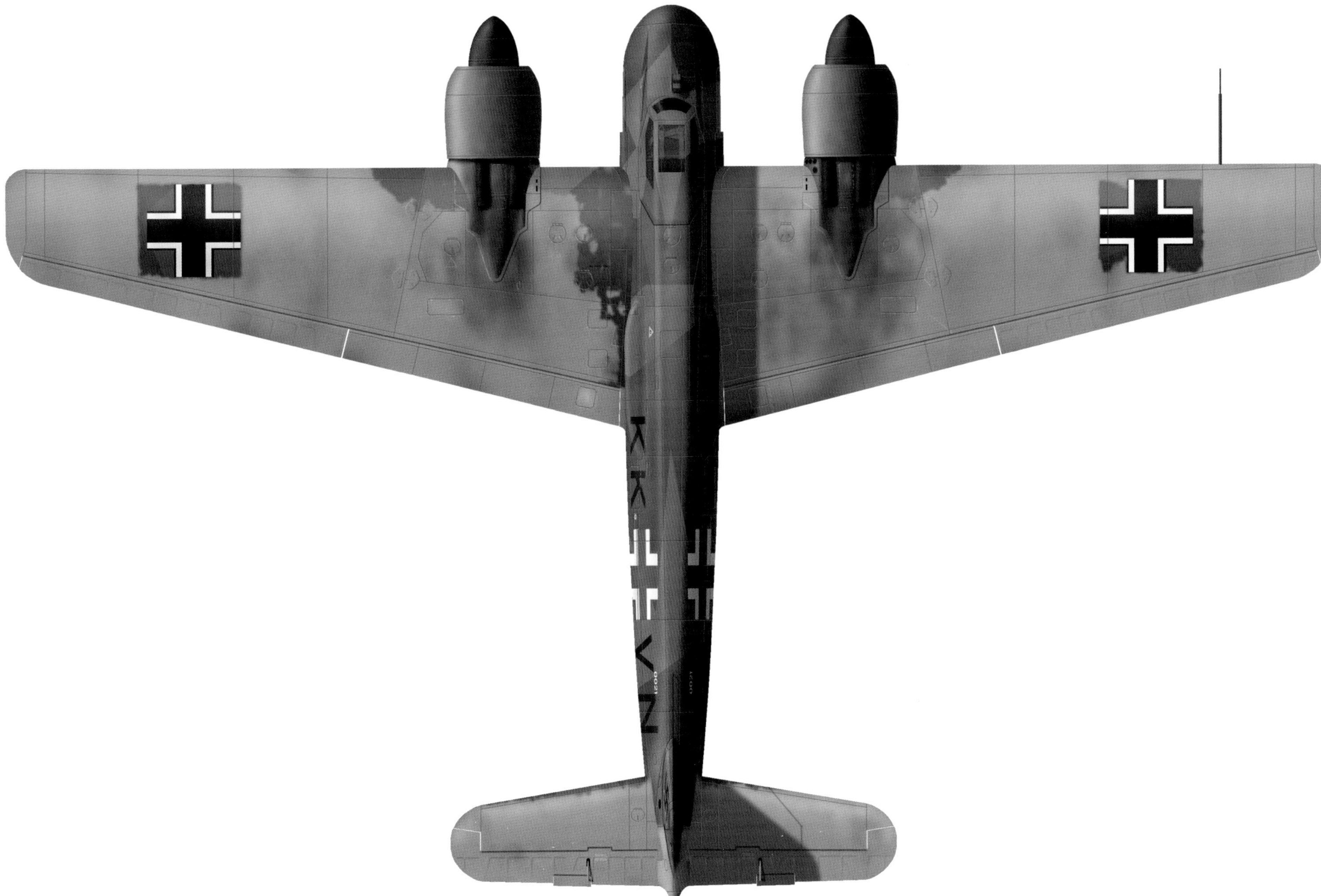

9

Hs 129B-1 W.Nr. 0155, SKZ KG+GM, 6.(Pz)/Sch.G 1.

Standard camouflage 70/71/65. Full Eastern Front markings (yellow front fuselage, fuselage band and bottom surfaces of wingtips), yellow spinner tips. Infantry assault badge on the fuselage nose. The machine is fitted with rack for additional 300 l-tank under fuselage. The a/c was shot down by AA near Volchansk on 24th June, 1942.

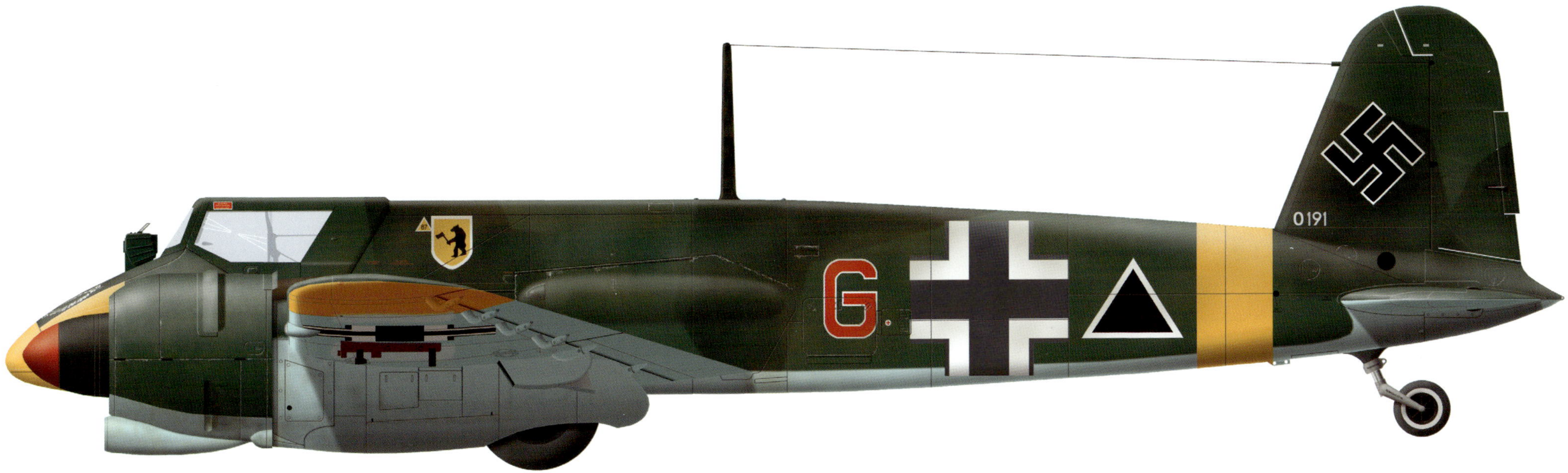

Hs 129B-1 W.Nr. 0191, SKZ NN, 5.(Pz)/Sch.G 1.

Standard camouflage 70/71/65. Full Eastern Front markings, blue spinner tips.
Infantry assault badge on the fuselage nose. SKZ on bottom wing surfaces painted over.
The a/c was shot down by AA fire at Konstantinovka on 23rd May, 1942.

11

Hs 129B-1 W.Nr. NN, SKZ NN, 13.(Pz.Jä.St.)/JG 51.

Standard camouflage 70/71/65 painted over with washable white paint.

Yellow front fuselage, incomplete yellow fuselage band, yellow spinner tips.

12

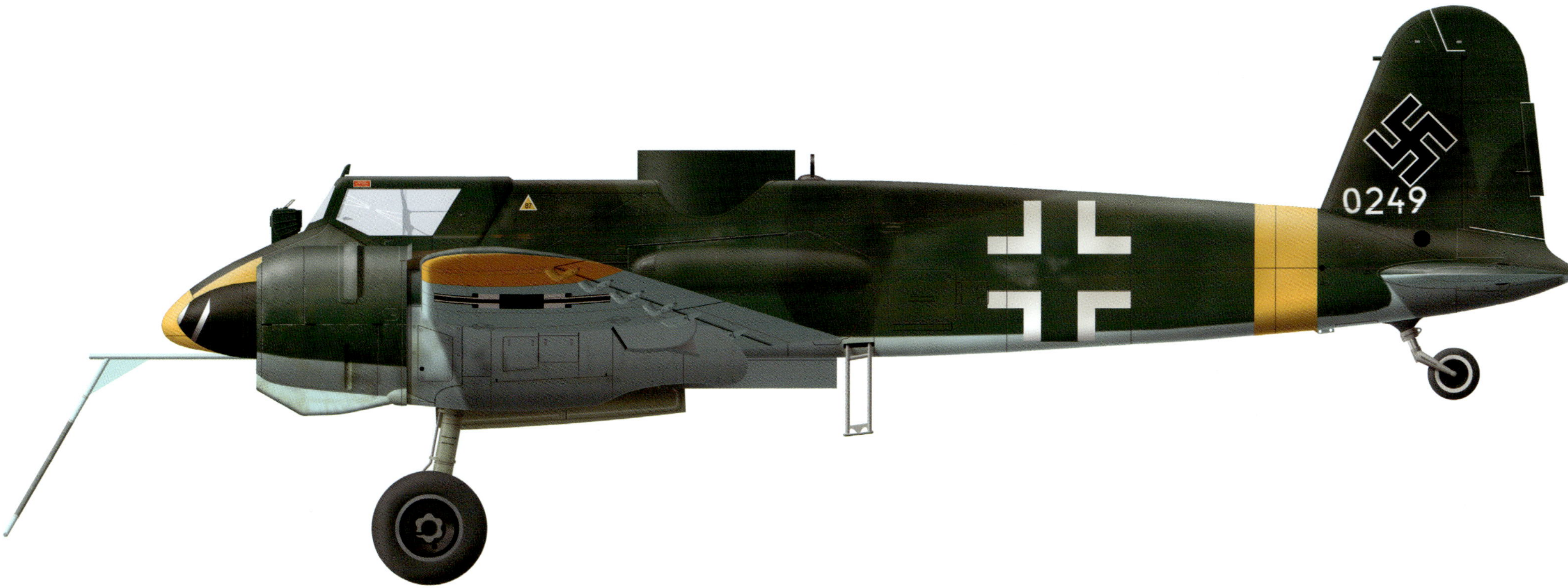

Hs 129B-2 W.Nr. 0249, SKZ NN.

Standard camouflage 70/71/65. Full Eastern Front markings, spinners with white spirals.
SKZ on bottom wing surfaces painted over.
The a/c was used for tests with six-barrel mortar SG 113 installed in the mid fuselage, and later served in II./SG 101.

13

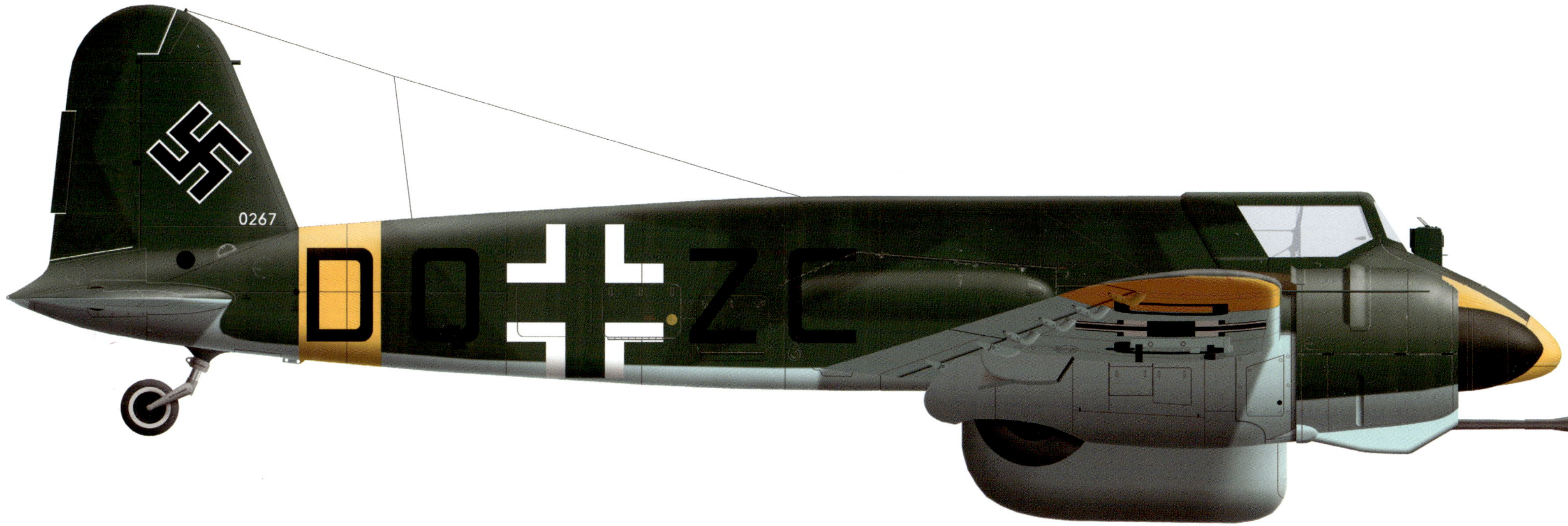

Hs 129B-2 W.Nr. 0267, SKZ DQ+ZC

Standard camouflage 70/71/65. Full Eastern Front markings.

The a/c was used for tests with 37-mm BK 3.7 cannon mounted under fuselage.

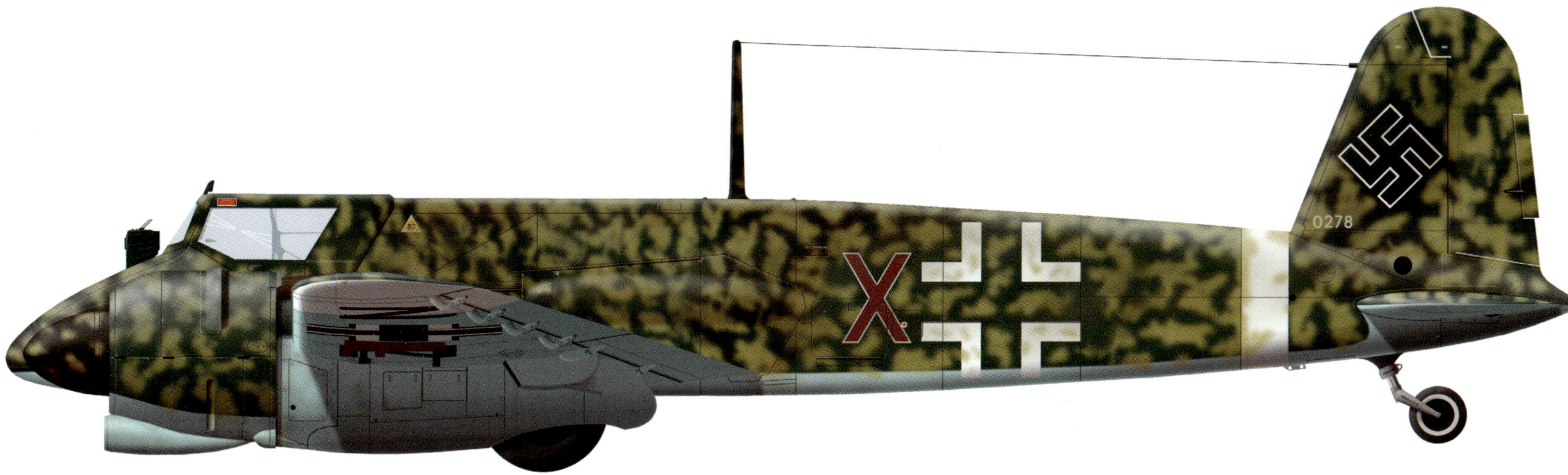

Hs 129B-2 W.Nr. 0278, SKZ DQ+ZN, 8.(Pz)/Sch.G 2.

Standard camouflage 70/71/65 almost entirely painted over with irregular light brown blotches (RLM 79?).
White fuselage band and bottom surfaces of wingtips. The fuselage letter "X" painted with dark red, possibly RLM 28 Weinrot.
The a/c was left by German troops at Al Aouina airfield and captured by Allies in February 1943.

15

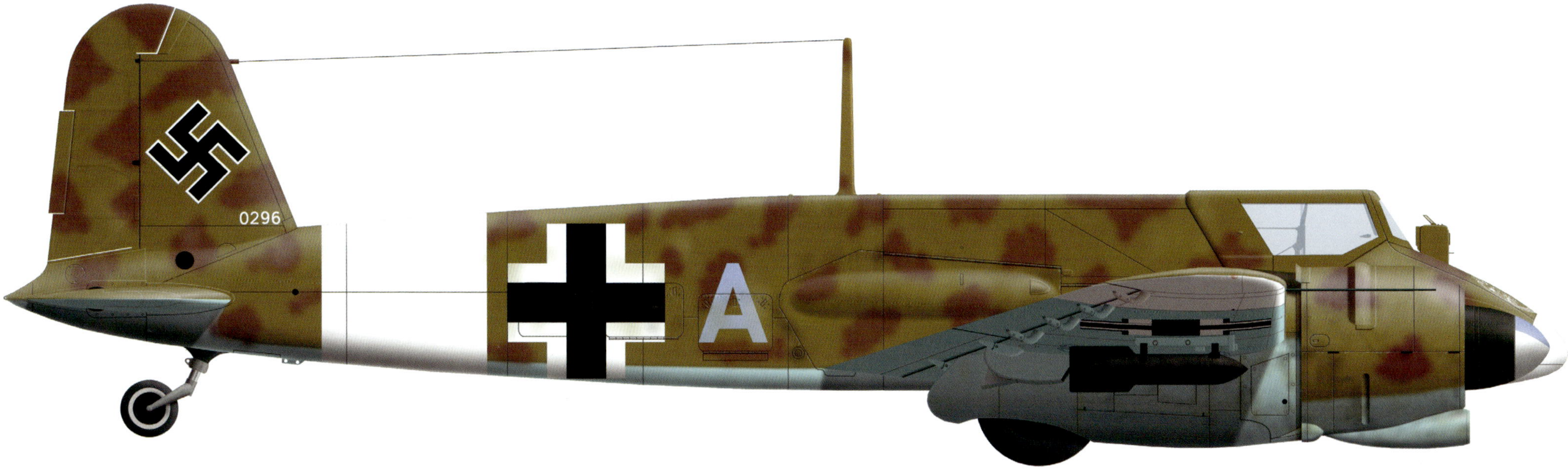

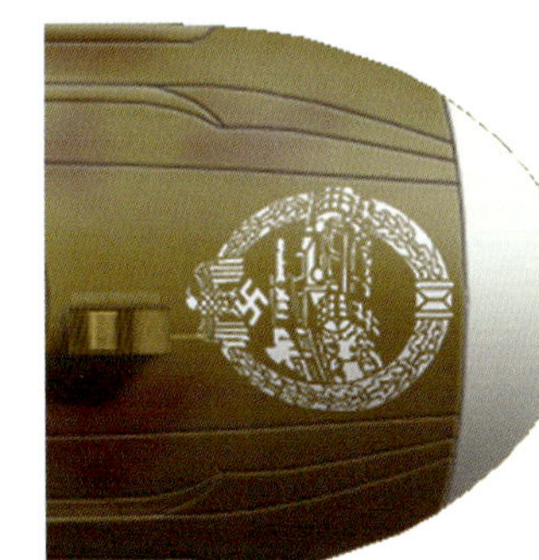

Hs 129B-2 W.Nr. 0296, SKZ GD+CF, 4.(Pz)/Sch.G 2.

Standard camouflage 70/71 painted over with African camouflage consisting of (supposedly) tank colours: Afrika Korps Gelb RAL 8000 and Rotbraun RAL 8017 (the Crashed Enemy Aircraft Report describes the camouflage as greenish-brown with purple blotches and a/m colours match the description almost exactly). White fuselage nose, fuselage band and bottom surfaces of wingtips. Tank assault badge on the fuselage nose. Spinner tips 2/3 white and 1/3 light blue, possibly RAF Light Mediterranean Blue. SKZ on bottom wing surfaces painted over. The a/c was destroyed and left by German troops at El Adem airfield and captured by Allies in early 1943.

Hs 129B-2 W.Nr. 0300, SKZ GD+CJ, 8.(Pz)/Sch.G 1.

Standard camouflage 70/71/65 painted over with washable white paint. Yellow fuselage band and bottom surfaces of wingtips.

On 9th May, 1943 the a/c was damaged (25%) by AA fire over Kerch and later repaired and transferred to 8./Rum.Sch.Gr.

17

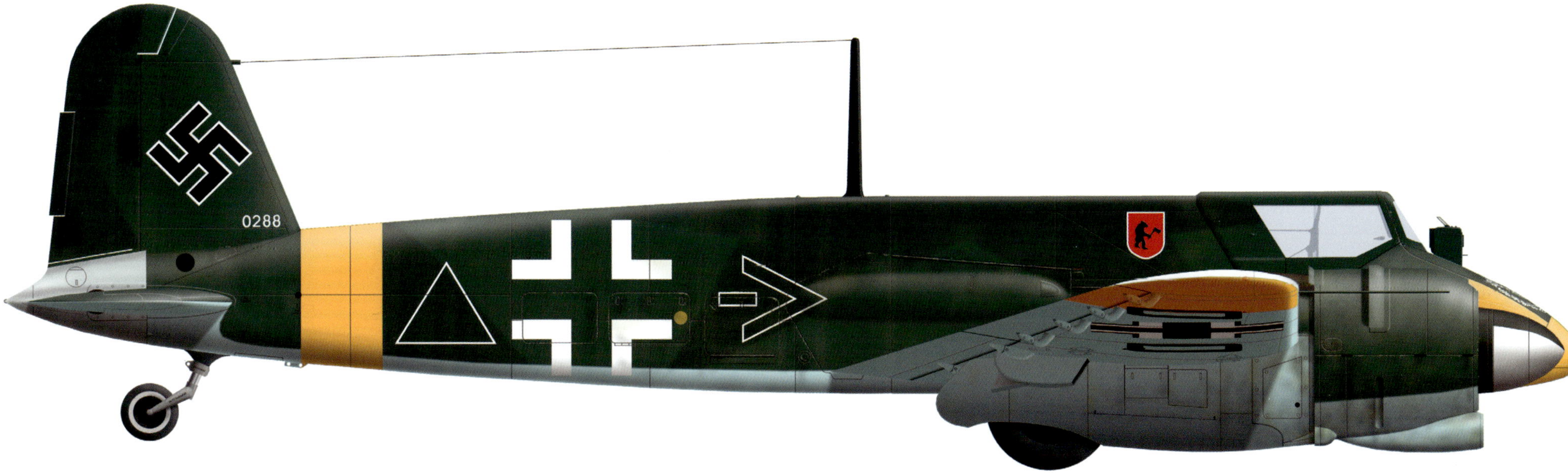

Hs 129B-2 W.Nr. 0288, SKZ DQ+ZX, Stab II./Sch.G 1.

Standard camouflage 70/71/65. Upper surfaces of outer wing sections painted white. Full Eastern Front markings, 1/3 of spinner tips white. Infantry assault badge on the fuselage nose. The Schlachtgeschwader triangle on the fuselage without black fill. The a/c was captured by Russians in unknown circumstances.

18

19

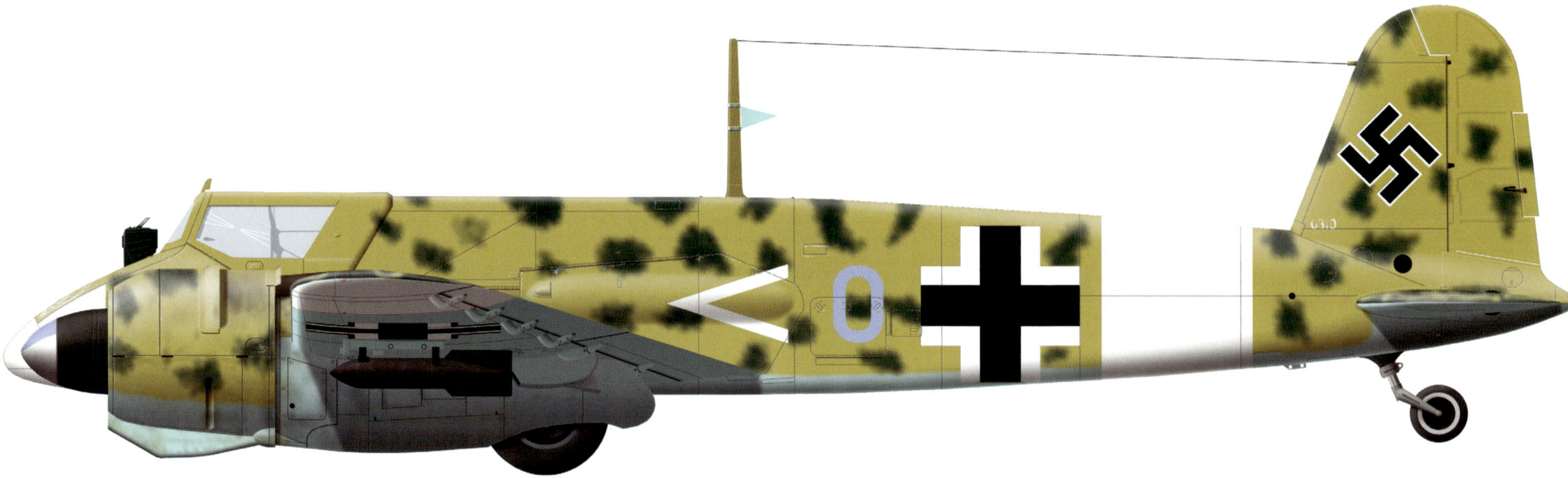

Hs 129B-2 W.Nr. 0310 (?), SKZ GD+CT, 4.(Pz)/Sch.G 2.

Standard camouflage 70/71 painted over with African camouflage consisting of RLM 79 Sandbraun with RLM 71 blotches.
White fuselage nose, fuselage band and bottom surfaces of wingtips. Silver infantry assault badge on the fuselage nose.
Spinner tips 2/3 white and 1/3 light blue. Three kill markings (two white and one red) on the port side of rudder. SKZ on bottom wing surfaces painted over.
The a/c was left by Germans at Castel Benito airfield and captured by Allies in February 1943.

Hs 129B-2 W.Nr. 0334, SKZ GG+EG, possibly II./Sch.G 1.

Standard camouflage 70/71/65 painted over with washable white paint. Full Eastern Front markings.

Hs 129B-2 W.Nr. 0342, SKZ GG+EO, 8.(Pz)/Sch.G 2.

Standard camouflage 70/71/65 painted over with wavy light brown lines (RLM 79?).
White fuselage band and bottom surfaces of wingtips. SKZ on bottom wing surfaces painted over.
The a/c was described in various publications as having the fuselage letter red “C” or “G”, but more careful look reveals the letter “O”!
The a/c was left damaged by German troops at Al Aouina airfield and captured by Allies in early 1943.

Hs 129B-2 W.Nr. 0366, SKZ VE+NO, 4.(Pz)/Sch.G 1.

Standard camouflage 70/71/65. Full Eastern Front markings, white spinner tips. Infantry assault badge on the fuselage nose.

The Schlachtgeschwader triangle on the fuselage without black fill.

On 13th May the a/c emergency-landed at Kerch due to technical fault, suffering 50% damage.

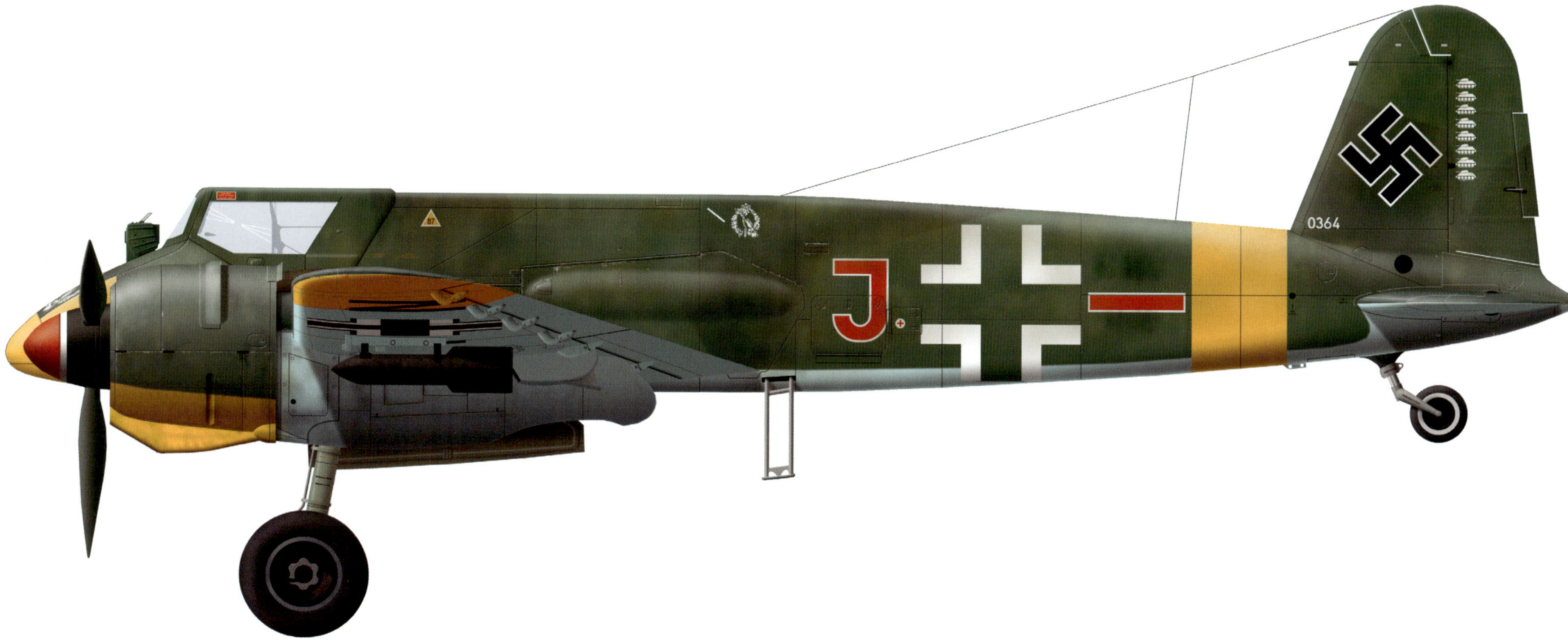

Hs 129B-2 W.Nr. 0364, SKZ GS+IN (or CC+IN), Hptm Rudolf-Heinz Ruffer, 8.(Pz)/Sch.G 1.

Standard camouflage 70/71/65, very worn and weathered.
Full Eastern Front markings, yellow bottom part of engine cowlings, red spinner tips with white band.
Infantry assault badge on the fuselage nose and fuselage centre. Seven kill markings on the port side of the rudder.
The a/c was shot down by AA fire on 27th May, 1943.

24

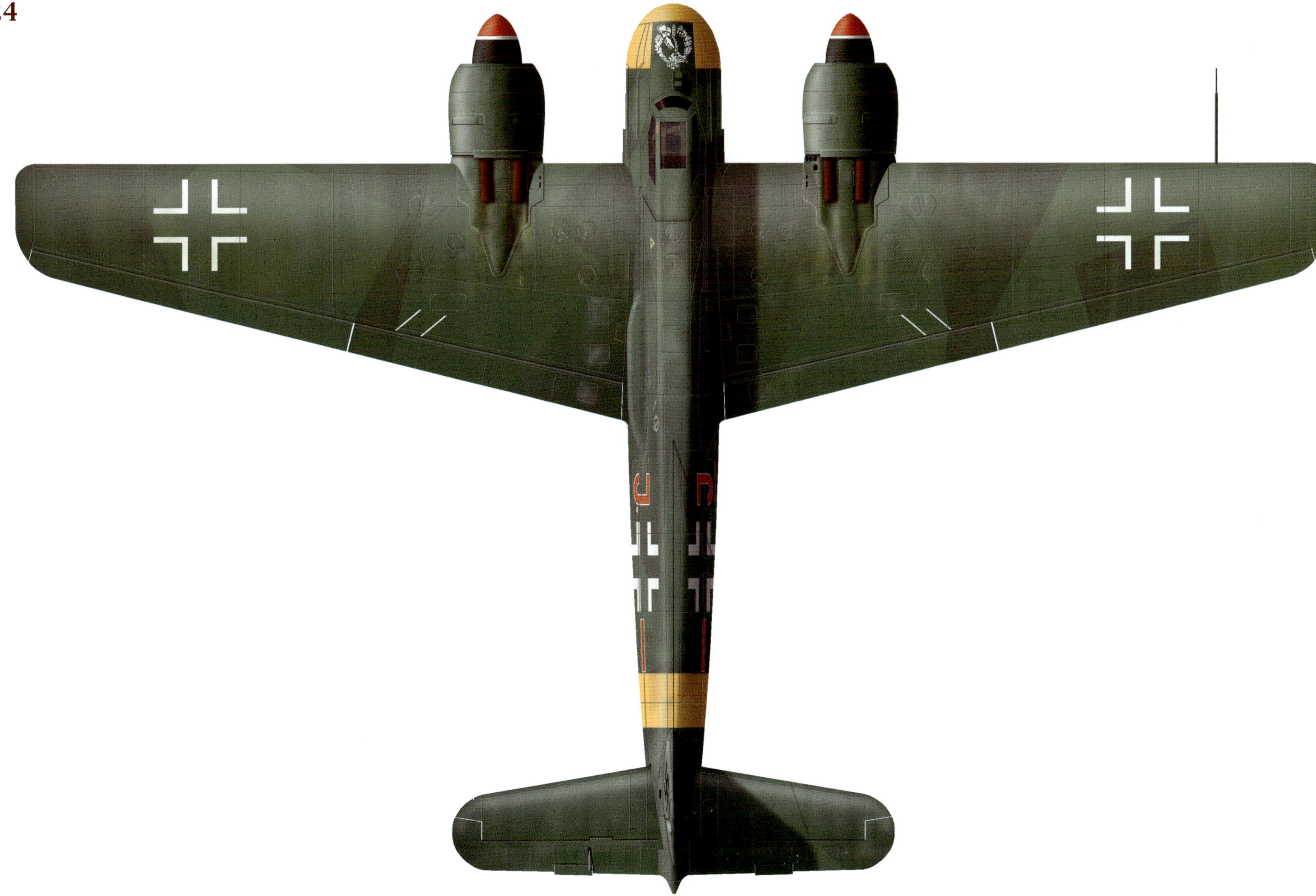

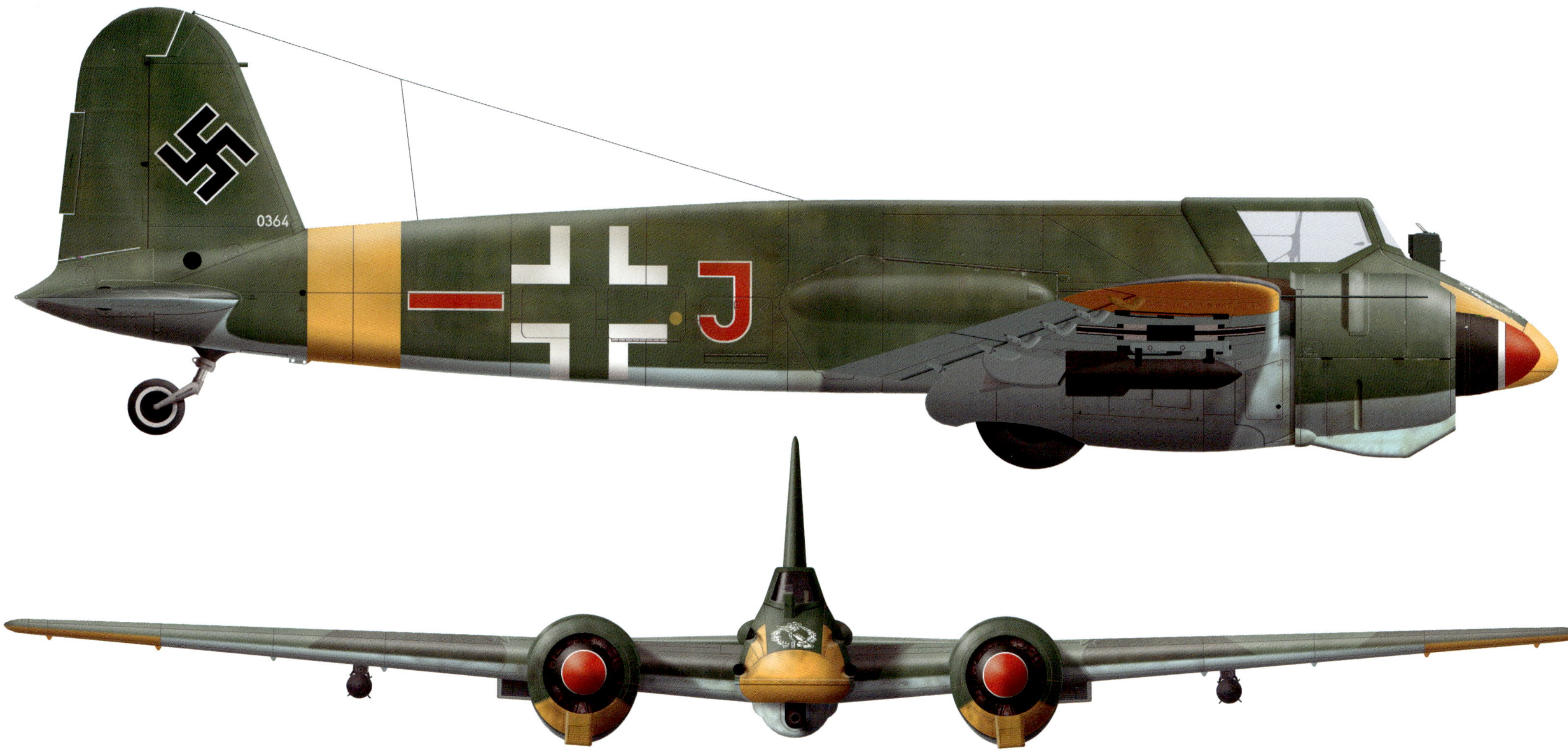

Hs 129B-2 W.Nr. 0364, SKZ GS+IN (or CC+IN), Hptm Rudolf-Heinz Ruffer, 8.(Pz)/Sch.G 1.

G
S
I
N

27

Hs 129B-2 W.Nr. 0350, SKZ GG+EW, 13.(Pz.Jä.St.)/JG 51.

Standard camouflage 70/71/65 partially painted over with washable white paint. Full Eastern Front markings, white spinner tips. Infantry assault badge on the fuselage nose. The a/c served subsequently in 8./Rum.Sch.Gr and was damaged by AAA fire (35%) on 4th October, 1943.

29

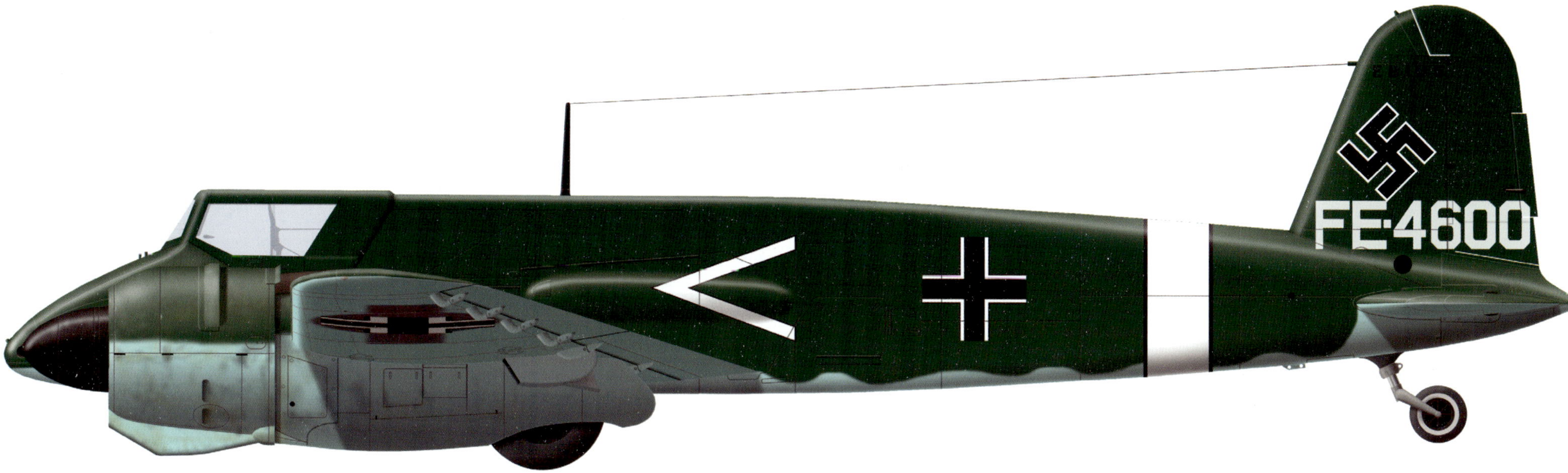

Hs 129B-2 W.Nr. 0385, SKZ PG+MV, 8.(Pz)/Sch.G 2, US No. FE-4600/EB105.

The machine is camouflaged probably with USAAF semi-gloss paints Green 7 and Light Blue 27, spinners are black. USAAF markings on wings painted over and replaced with German crosses. The a/c was damaged by AA fire (20%) on 7th April, 1943, left by Germans at Al Aouina airfield and captured by US troops. During one of test flights in US the a/c piloted by Lt Kenneth Almond emergency-landed due to lack of fuel at Gallatin, Tennessee on 24th July, 1945 suffering moderate damage.

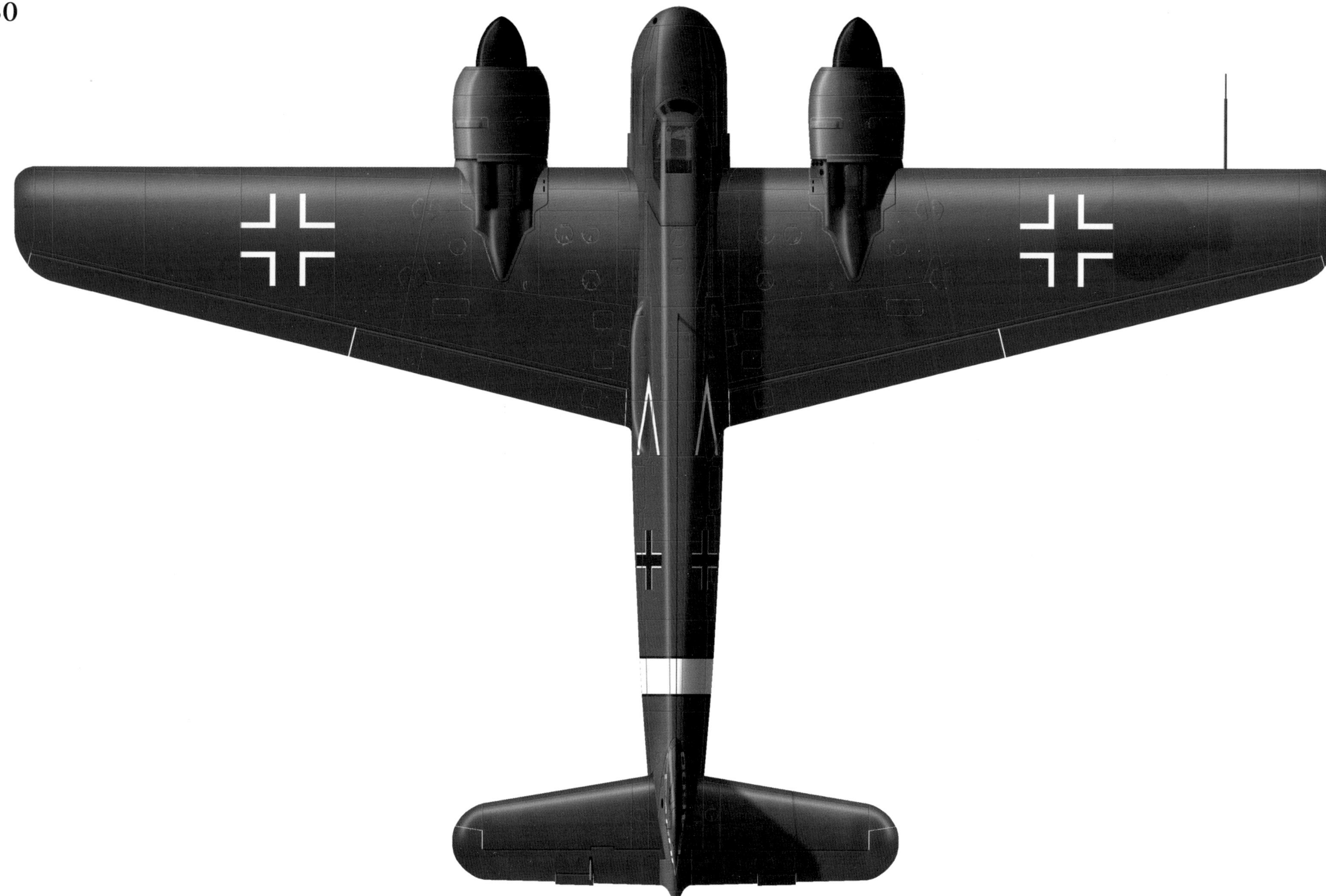

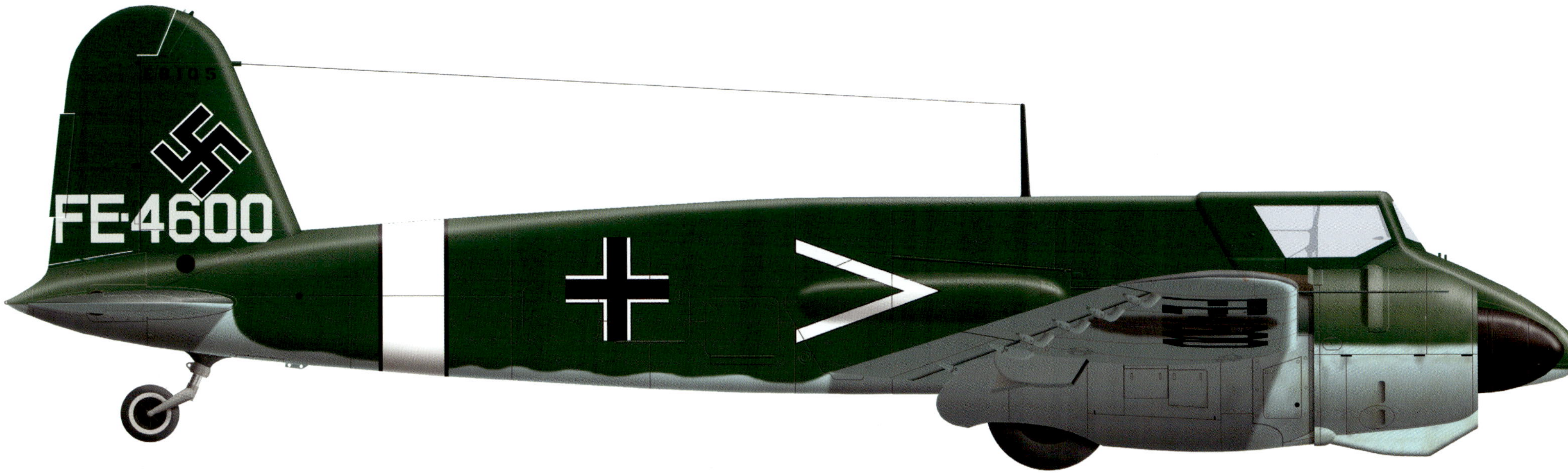

Hs 129B-2 W.Nr. 0385, SKZ PG+MV, 8.(Pz)/Sch.G 2, US No. FE-4600/EB105.

FE-4600

33

Hs 129B-2 W.Nr. 0375, SKZ PG+ML, 8.(Pz)/Sch.G 1.

Standard camouflage 70/71/65. Full Eastern Front markings.

On 25th July, 1943 the a/c crashed during taxiing on airfield at Karachev suffering 40% damage.

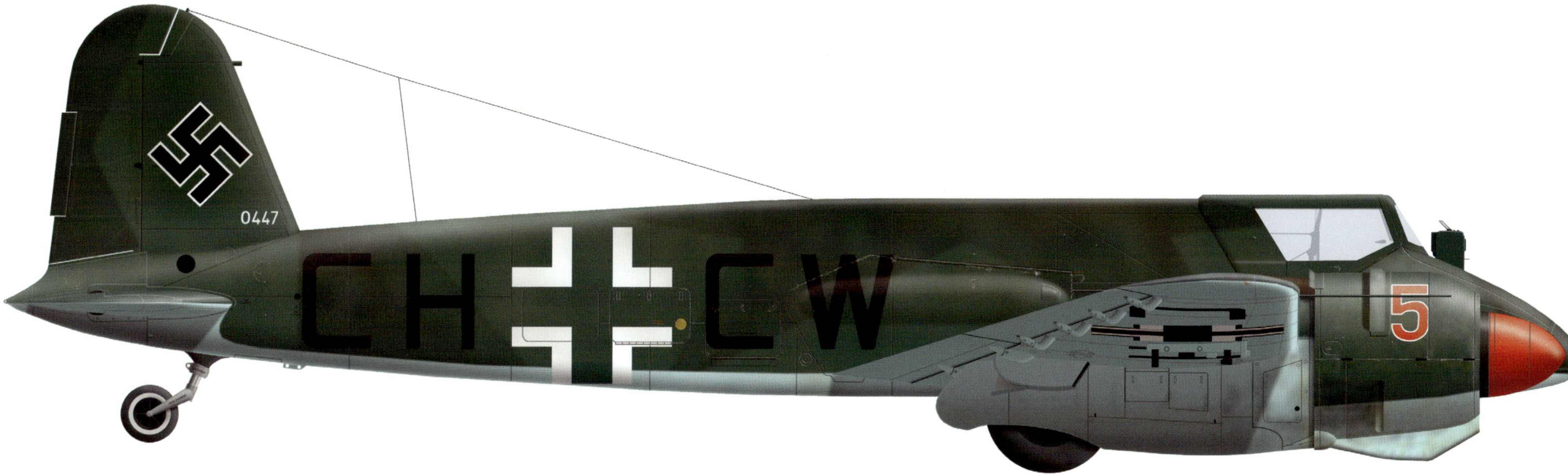

Hs 129B-2 W.Nr. 0447 (?), SKZ CH+CW (?), 2./SG 101.

Standard camouflage 70/71/65, red spinners.

35

Hs 129B-2 W.Nr. 140508, SKZ DO+XU, 8.(Pz)/Sch.G 1.

Standard camouflage 70/71/65, rather worn and weathered. Full Eastern Front markings, yellow bottom part of engine cowlings, red spinner tips with white band.
Infantry assault badge on the fuselage nose.
The a/c was shot by AA fire on 16th July, 1943.

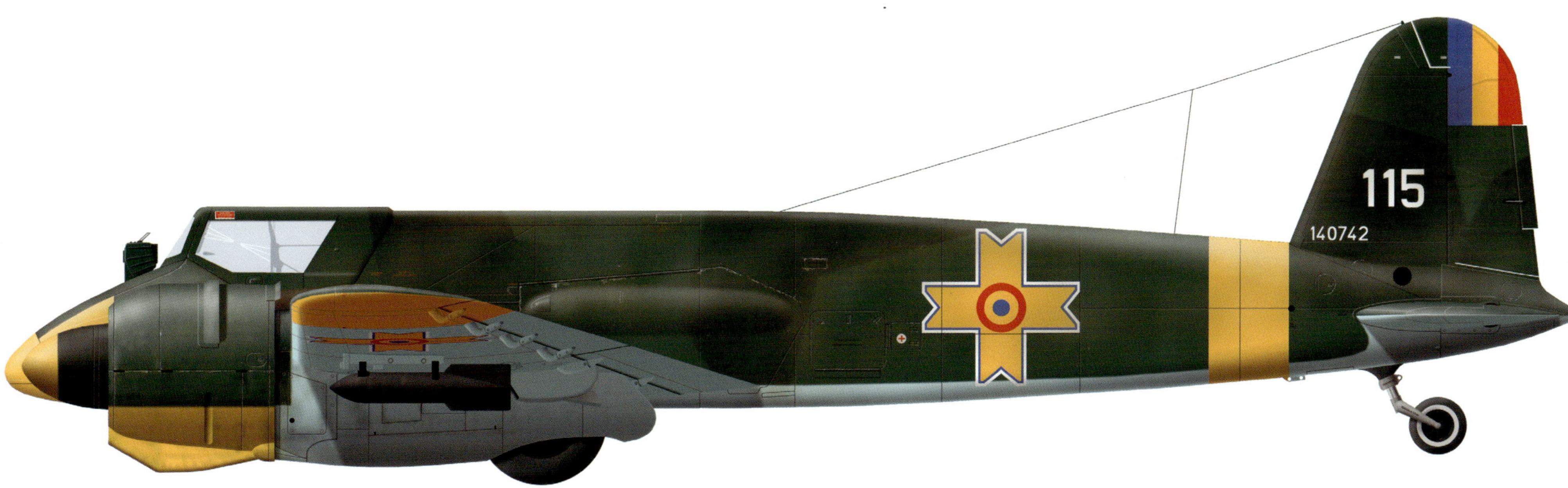

Hs 129B-2 W.Nr. 140742, SKZ GL+PV, 8./Rum.Sch.Gr.

Standard camouflage 70/71/65. Full Eastern Front markings, yellow bottom part of engine cowlings, yellow spinner tips. SKZ on bottom wing surfaces painted over. The a/c was damaged by bombs (20%) on Kramatorskaya airfield on 19th August, 1943.

Hs 129B-2 W.Nr. 140494, SKZ DO+XG.

Standard camouflage 70/71/65, full Eastern Front markings, yellow bottom part of engine cowlings.

The a/c was used for tests with 75-mm BK 7.5 cannon.

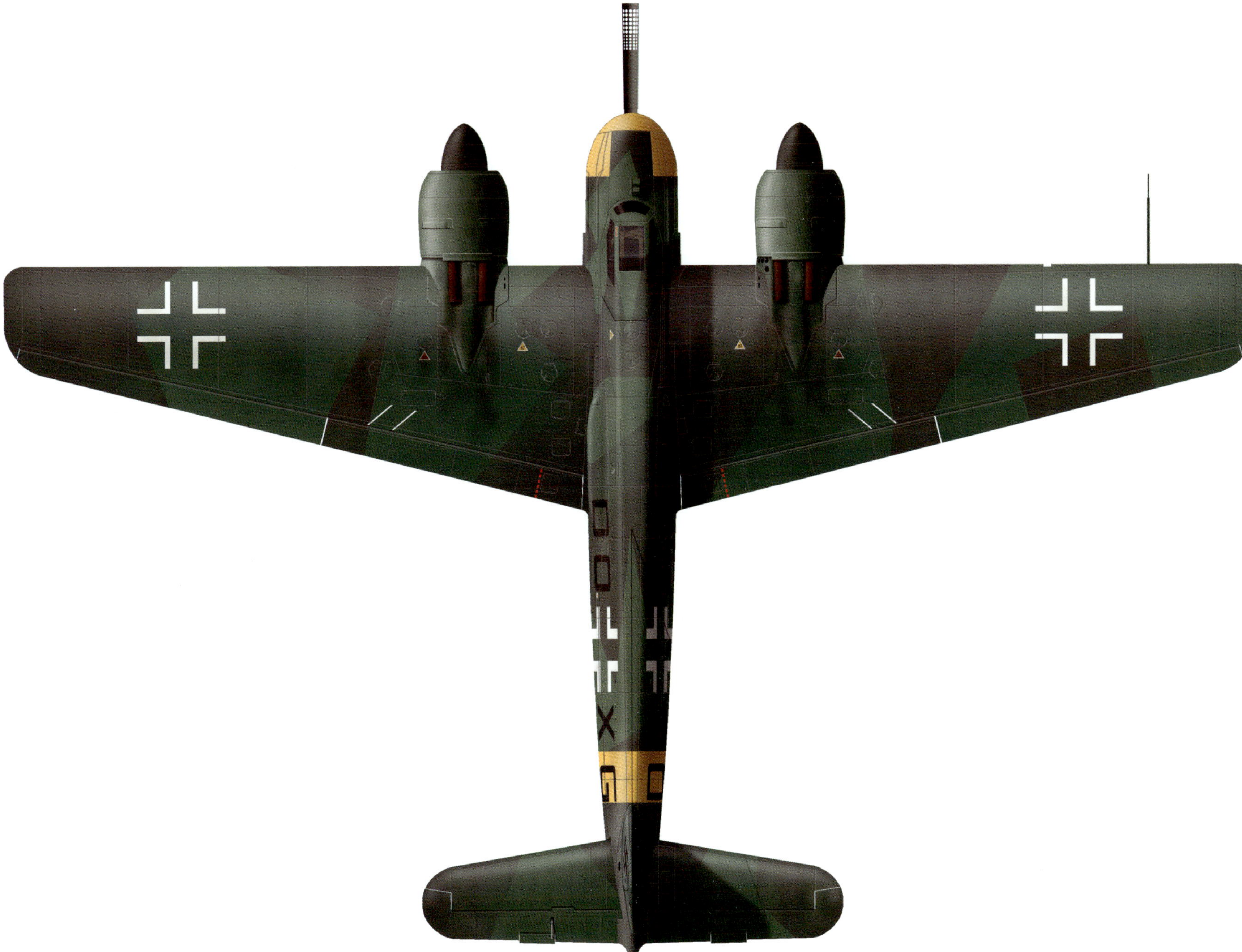

Hs 129B-2 W.Nr. 140494, SKZ DO+XG.

D
O
X
G

41

Hs 129B-2 W.Nr. 140809, 8./Rum.Sch.Gr.

Standard camouflage 70/71/65 partially painted over with washable white paint. Full Eastern Front markings, yellow bottom part of engine cowlings, yellow spinner tips. SKZ on bottom wing surfaces painted over.
The a/c piloted by Capt. Alfred Conrad crashed at Lepetikha airfield due to pilot's error, killing Conrand instantly.

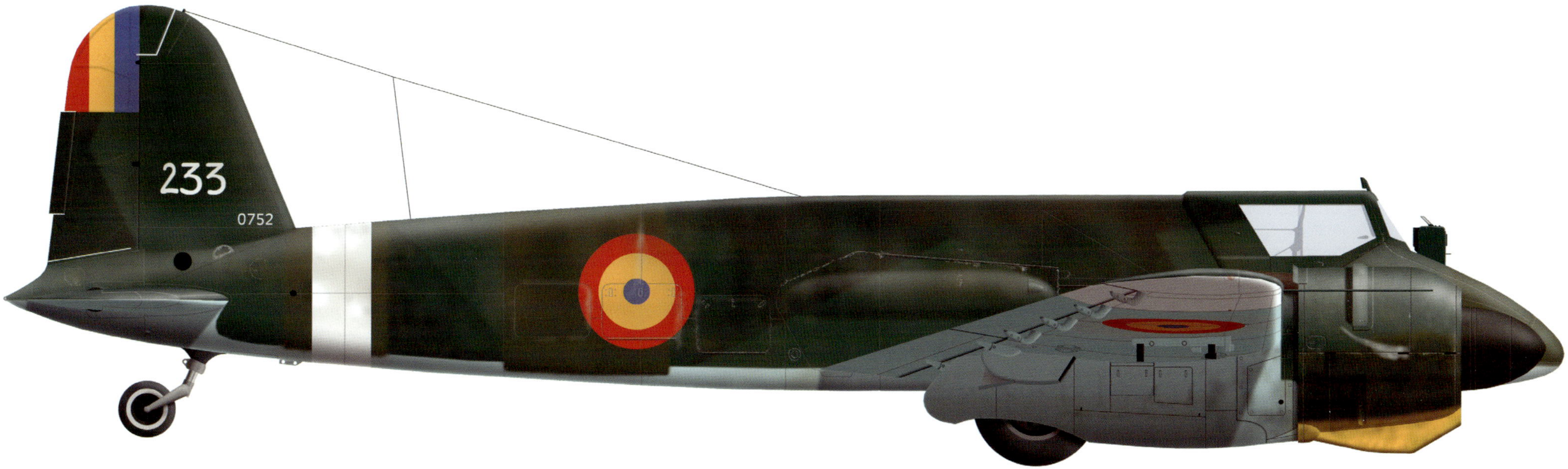

Hs 129B-2 W.Nr. 140752, Escadrila 41 asalt/Grupul 8.

Standard camouflage 70/71/65. Yellow bottom part of engine cowlings, previous Romanian markings painted over with dark olive paint (?) and replaced with cockades of pre-war type, white fuselage band. SKZ on bottom wing surfaces painted over.
2/Lt Alexandru Nicolau defected with this a/c to the Germans on 13th January, 1945.

Published in Poland in 2019
by STRATUS sp.j.
Po. Box 123,
27-600 Sandomierz 1, Poland
e-mail: office@mmpbooks.biz
as
MMPBooks,

e-mail: office@mmpbooks.biz

ISBN
978-83-65958-27-3

Editor in chief
Roger Wallsgrove

Editorial Team
Bartłomiej Belcarz
Robert Pęczkowski
Artur Juszczak

Colour profiles
Krzysztof Wołowski

DTP
Stratus sp.j.

Printed by
Drukarnia Diecezjalna,
ul. Żeromskiego 4,
27-600 Sandomierz
www.wds.pl
marketing@wds.pl

PRINTED IN POLAND

Introduction, continued.

the B-0 started in the last month of 1940. the first main series airframes changed to the new 'B' standards were the 16 A-1s (W. Nr. 0016-0031) already in production, which were renamed B-0s. The B-0 batch was finished in January 1942. Next on the production line were the ten initial B-0s (W. Nr. 0151-0160), also under construction, now upgraded to B-1 standards. These were to be followed by 50 planned B-1s (W.Nr. 0161-0210), which would have concluded the B-1 series. This number would also fulfil the existing RLM order calling for 60 improved Schlachtflugzeuge. However, only the first 40 airframes were eventually completed as B-1s (W. Nr. 0161-0200), as the last ten were upgraded to the new B-2 standards. The 50th and last B-1 (W. Nr. 0200) rolled off the production line in mid-May 1942. By then, production shifted from the Schönefeld main centre (Werk I) to Henschel Flugzeug-Werke's newer and larger Johannisthal Plant (Werk II), where mass production was planned. The first B-1 was delivered in December 1941, being followed by three in January, another three in February and six in March. In March, Hs 129B-1 production lagged behind compared to Lieferplan 222 by 19 aircraft. This was due to "significant changes in production". April production jumped to 31, well exceeding the planned 16 aircraft. Yet, the balance owing was still four aircraft.

The first main series airframes changed to the new 'B' standards were the 16 A-1s (W. Nr. 0016-0031) already in production, which were renamed B-0s. The B-0 batch was finished in January 1942. Next on the production line were the ten initial B-0s (W. Nr. 0151-0160), also under construction, now upgraded to B-1 standards. These were to be followed by 50 planned B-1s (W.Nr. 0161-0210), which would have concluded the B-1 series. This number would also fulfil the existing RLM order calling for 60 improved *Schlachtflugzeuge*. However, only the first 40 airframes were eventually completed as B-1s (W. Nr. 0161-0200), as the last ten were upgraded to the new B-2 standards. The 50th and last B-1 (W. Nr. 0200) rolled off the production line in mid-May 1942. By then, production shifted from the Schönefeld main centre (*Werk* I) to Henschel *Flugzeug-Werke*'s newer and larger Johannisthal Plant (*Werk* II), where mass production was planned. The first B-1 was delivered in December 1941, being followed by three in January, another three in February and six in March. In March, Hs 129B-1 production lagged behind compared to *Lieferplan* 222 by 19 aircraft. This was due to "*significant changes in production*". April production jumped to 31, well exceeding the planned 16 aircraft. Yet, the balance owing was still four aircraft.

Even before the first series B-1 was handed over, the RLM had issued a new purchase order on 15 October 1941. Initially, the order called for 250 tropicalised Hs 129B-1s (W. Nr. 0201-0450). However, in April 1942 this modification was dropped and the actual specification changed to a new and further improved sub-type, the B-2, with an option of up to 1000 additional aircraft. Although the B-2 was to be powered by the same readily-available Gnôme-Rhône 14M engines (because the series-produced Hs 129s still did not fully meet requirements) the RLM requested that from W. Nr. 0450 onwards a new, more powerful and reliable, yet unspecified, engine type had to be fitted to the unchanged airframes.

With series production well under way, the Henschel design team, led by Dipl.-Ing. Nicolaus, continued to work on improving their brainchild. By May 1942, they had formulated a number of minor modifications, aimed at improving the design's weaknesses, which had emerged as a result of flight trials and the introduction in combat service of the first Hs 129B-1s on the Eastern Front.

Although none of these modifications was radical, but rather details, they resulted in a change to a new sub-type, the Hs 129B-2. This was to be the main Hs 129 sub-type, representing over 90% of the total Hs 129 production run. Immediately upon approval, the modifications were incorporated into the airframes under construction, which were the last ten B-1 units (W.Nr. 0201-0210), which thus were renamed B-2s. The first B-2 (W.Nr. 0201) rolled out in mid-May 1942.

Excerpts from the book: Henschel Hs 129, ISBN: 978-83-89450-46-3 by Dénes Bernád.